Geol
New York

PENS
and
NEEDLES

PENS and

Literary Caricatures by

Selected and Introduced by

NEEDLES

DAVID LEVINE

JOHN UPDIKE

Gambit
INCORPORATED
Boston
1969

DAVID LEVINE, *par lui-même*

The man above knows what he looks like from the side; this is extremely rare. Rarer still are caricaturists of his caliber. Their signature certifies an epoch. In 1963, when the newly founded *New York Review of Books* began to publish the drawings of David Levine, the art of caricature in America was quiescent; the theatrical cartoons of Al Frueh in *The New Yorker* had ceased, Al Hirschfeld had become primarily a decorator of advertisements, and William Auerbach-Levy, the most artful of all, had rounded off his career with an elegant album entitled— a question he had too often heard—"Is That Me?" These men had followed the linear tradition of Ralph Barton and Max Beerbohm; economy was the soul of their wit, and their mood, as they reduced the features of this or that celebrity to a cunning black-and-white design, partook of the genial mood of showbiz.

Levine, instead, flung himself in a fury of crosshatching upon his subjects. His style looked past Beerbohm to the three-dimensional grotesques of Daumier and Tenniel. No weary pucker or complacent bulge of physiognomy could slip through the supple net of his penstrokes, and every corner of the face—that vulnerable patch between the eyebrows, the unseemly area behind the chin, the mute folds of the ears—was brought into a focus whose keenness transcended the mild demands of "humor." On the gray expanse of the *New York Review* pages his etched homunculi seemed astoundingly *there;* one wanted to pick them up and put them on the shelf. Now, in the form of this book, one can.

Our selection concentrates upon literary figures. Drawn in fortnightly installments to illustrate topical book reviews, the gallery of modern authors approaches completeness. Mann and Borges are missing, and one wonders what Levine would do with Salinger's sad handsomeness or Kierkegaard's bent beauty. But how good it is to know that Gide has no top to his head, and that Truman Capote has no chin, resting, like Baudelaire, within his bowtie like an egg in an eggcup. Levine is not so much an observer as a visionary. Working principally from photographs, he evolves a concept, a monstrous breathing idea. His grasp of this idea deepens with time; of the two versions of Malraux in this volume, the one is a caricature and the other is a caricature of a caricature. Of the three Becketts, the smallest and earliest has the innocence of wit; it puns the man and buzzard. This simile is absorbed and heightened in the alarming metaphor of the profile, with its drastically eroded cheek, its delirious pinpoint eye, its incredible chopping-knife of an ear. And the lava contours and volcanic turtle-neck of the third drawing seem gouged from chaos and quite intimidate any thought of satire. Levine's evolving style (see also the two of Galbraith, the two of Orwell) re-invents the gargoyle, that antidote to the angel and necessary adjunct to a complete humanism. All we humans, beneath the faces that would proclaim for each a separate individuality, share the worse-than-simian weirdness of thinking reeds. Mankind is a riddle it takes the Gothic style to pose.

Since Levine, as clairvoyant, has liberated himself from the physical presence of the subject, the living and the dead are the same to him, and with uncanny authority he conveys, out of fudged old portraits and stylized prints, the essence of the immortals. Take Browning's wonderfully astute, plump, and conceited left hand; or Ben Franklin's cherry-nosed, finger-snapping display of pragmatic pep; or Casanova's evidently numbing virility. The artist discovers a surprising dandyish sneer on the time-softened face of John Milton, and elicits from the noseless bust of Catullus, at the farthest rim of Caricature's reach, the agonized satyr's howl that resounds through imperial Rome. One looks forward to, yet rather dreads, Levine's inevitable cartoon of Jesus. Unless this is already it:

Our artist was born in 1926 in Brooklyn, where he still lives. He has been quoted as describing himself as "a painter supported by a hobby—satirical drawings." As a painter he is representational and has been described, by John Canaday, as "a legitimate anachronism." In his comic art also he displays somewhat anachronistic qualities. Besides offering us the delight of recognition, his drawings comfort us, in an exacerbated and potentially desperate age, with the sense of a watching presence, an eye informed by an intelligence that has not panicked, a comic art ready to encapsulate the latest apparitions of publicity (Twiggy inspires a drawing too lovely to omit) as well as those historical devils who haunt our unease. Levine is one of America's assets. In a confusing time, he bears witness. In a shoddy time, he does good work. Here he is.

John Updike

CONTENTS

The New World

BENJAMIN FRANKLIN

RALPH WALDO EMERSON

EDGAR ALLAN POE

NATHANIEL HAWTHORNE

MARK TWAIN

(with Huckleberry Finn)

6

Mark Twain

STEPHEN CRANE

8

HENRY JAMES

THEODORE DREISER

SINCLAIR LEWIS

LEWIS *(with Dorothy Thompson)*

11

H. L. MENCKEN

THEODORE DREISER and H. L. MENCKEN

THOMAS WOLFE

GERTRUDE STEIN

WILLIAM FAULKNER

F. Scott Fitzgerald

F. Scott Fitzgerald and Ernest Hemingway

ERNEST HEMINGWAY

17

HENRY MILLER

JOHN O'HARA

18

KATHERINE ANNE PORTER

T. S. Eliot

ROBERT FROST

Marianne Moore

W. H. Auden

EDMUND WILSON

24

EDMUND WILSON

MARSHALL McLUHAN

26

LIONEL TRILLING

DWIGHT MACDONALD

ARTHUR M. SCHLESINGER, JR.

JOHN KENNETH GALBRAITH

29

MARY McCARTHY

WILLIAM STYRON

30

JACK KEROUAC

TRUMAN CAPOTE

31

NORMAN MAILER, ROBERT LOWELL, DWIGHT MACDONALD

Robert Lowell

NORMAN MAILER

NORMAN MAILER

ARTHUR MILLER   TENNESSEE WILLIAMS

EDWARD ALBEE

37

Isaac Bashevis Singer

Bernard Malamud

38

SAUL BELLOW

39

VLADIMIR NABOKOV

40

VLADIMIR NABOKOV

SUSAN SONTAG

JAMES BALDWIN

LEROI JONES

43

JOHN UPDIKE

44

PHILIP ROTH

45

The Continent

CATULLUS

LEONARDO DA VINCI

49

BLAISE PASCAL

50

CASANOVA

51

JEAN BAPTISTE RACINE

MARQUIS DE SADE

VOLTAIRE

53

Jean Jacques Rousseau

Honoré de Balzac

ALEXANDER PUSHKIN

JOHANN WOLFGANG VON GOETHE

55

LEO TOLSTOY

56

ANTON CHEKHOV

FYODOR DOSTOEVSKY

KARL MARX

KARL MARX *(with Georg Wilhelm Friedrich Hegel)*

HENRIK IBSEN

GUSTAVE FLAUBERT

60

ARTHUR RIMBAUD

CHARLES BAUDELAIRE

61

COMTE ROBERT DE MONTESQUIEU

MARCEL PROUST

Jean-Paul Sartre

SIMONE DE BEAUVOIR

André Gide

ALBERT CAMUS

NATHALIE SARRAUTE

67

ANDRÉ MALRAUX

COLETTE

JEAN GENET

70

LOUIS-FERDINAND CÉLINE

71

SAMUEL BECKETT

72

SAMUEL BECKETT

73

CESARE PAVESE

ALBERTO MORAVIA

ITALO SVEVO

75

SIGMUND FREUD

RAINER MARIA RILKE

FRANZ KAFKA

KARL JASPERS

78

BERTOLT BRECHT

GÜNTER GRASS

Ludwig Wittgenstein

80

ISAK DINESEN

ARTHUR KOESTLER

S. Y. Agnon

Isaac Babel

VLADIMIR MAYAKOVSKY

84

Maxim Gorky

ILYA EHRENBURG

86

MIKHAIL SHOLOKHOV

87

BORIS PASTERNAK

ANDREI VOZNESENSKY

YEVGENY YEVTUSHENKO

Andrei Sinyavsky

90

ALEXANDER SOLZHENITSYN

The British

WILLIAM SHAKESPEARE

FRANCIS BACON

Isaac Newton

JOHN MILTON

JONATHAN SWIFT

ALEXANDER POPE

Edward Gibbon

WILLIAM WORDSWORTH

WILLIAM BLAKE

S<small>AMUEL</small> T<small>AYLOR</small> C<small>OLERIDGE</small>

103

LORD BYRON

JOHN KEATS

PERCY BYSSHE SHELLEY

105

ROBERT BROWNING

ALFRED TENNYSON

106

WILLIAM MORRIS

107

GEORGE ELIOT

CHARLES DICKENS

THOMAS CARLYLE

110

CARDINAL JOHN HENRY NEWMAN

More blue, that's it
Turner, now a touch of
naples
that's
it a
drop
of water
now
blot
it,
try
scratching
on the left.
Clumsy
can't you
leave the
paper
here and
there? Did
you ever
think of
going to
Venice?

JOHN RUSKIN

LEWIS CARROLL

EDWARD LEAR

BEATRIX POTTER

RUDYARD KIPLING

114

BENJAMIN DISRAELI

(with Queen Victoria)

THOMAS HARDY

115

Aubrey Beardsley

Oscar Wilde

117

GEORGE BERNARD SHAW

JOSEPH CONRAD

118

RUPERT BROOKE

MAX BEERBOHM

Ford Madox Ford

Arnold Bennett

SOMERSET MAUGHAM

E. M. FORSTER

H. G. WELLS

SIDNEY AND BEATRICE WEBB

BERTRAND RUSSELL

125

WILLIAM BUTLER YEATS

126

W. B. Yeats, D. H. Lawrence, Wyndham Lewis,

T. S. Eliot, Ezra Pound

LEONARD WOOLF

VIRGINIA WOOLF

128

LYTTON STRACHEY

JAMES JOYCE

130

JAMES JOYCE

ROBERT GRAVES

EVELYN WAUGH

132

D. H. LAWRENCE

SEAN O'CASEY

JOHN MAYNARD KEYNES

WINSTON CHURCHILL

135

J. R. R. Tolkien

ARNOLD TOYNBEE

H. R. TREVOR-ROPER

GRAHAM GREENE

Dame Edith Sitwell

DORIS LESSING

C. P. SNOW

LAWRENCE DURRELL

WILLIAM GOLDING

ANGUS WILSON

BRENDAN BEHAN

142

ANTHONY POWELL

NOEL COWARD

DYLAN THOMAS

GEORGE ORWELL

Twiggy

THE BEATLES

147

INDEX

149

BLACK
SMOKE

BLACK SMOKE

AFRICAN AMERICANS AND THE
UNITED STATES OF BARBECUE

ADRIAN MILLER

A Ferris and Ferris Book

THE UNIVERSITY OF NORTH CAROLINA PRESS

Chapel Hill

This book was published under the
MARCIE COHEN FERRIS AND WILLIAM R. FERRIS IMPRINT
of the University of North Carolina Press.

© 2021 Adrian Miller
All rights reserved
Manufactured in the United States of America
Designed by Richard Hendel
Set in Chaparral and Publicity Gothic
by Tseng Information Systems, Inc.

The University of North Carolina Press has been
a member of the Green Press Initiative since 2003.

Cover photograph courtesy of Andrew Thomas Lee,
www.andrewthomaslee.com.

Library of Congress Cataloging-in-Publication Data
Names: Miller, Adrian, author.
Title: Black smoke : African Americans and the United States of barbecue / Adrian Miller.
Description: Chapel Hill : The University of North Carolina Press, [2021] |
"A Ferris and Ferris book." | Includes bibliographical references and index.
Identifiers: LCCN 2020051252 | ISBN 9781469662800 (cloth) |
ISBN 9781469662817 (ebook)
Subjects: LCSH: Barbecuing—United States. | African American
cooking. | African American cooks.
Classification: LCC TX840.B3 M529 2021 | DDC 641.7/60973—dc23
LC record available at https://lccn.loc.gov/2020051252

The recipe for Spicy Grilled Kebabs (Dibi Hausa) © Pierre Thiam.
Reprinted by permission from *YOLELE! Recipes from the Heart of Senegal*
by Pierre Thiam © 2008 Lake Isle Press, Inc.

For celebrated,

underappreciated, and

undiscovered

Black barbecuers . . .

everywhere.

CONTENTS

ILLUSTRATIONS

FIGURES

COLOR PLATES (*Following page 178*)

RECIPES

SIDEBARS